THE
METHOD

5 INQUIRY STEPS TO
ENLIGHTENMENT

KYLE HOOBIN

SIMHA SAT PUBLISHING

Published by
Simha Sat Publishing
www.simhasatpublishing.com
Printed in the United States of America

The Method
5 Inquiry Steps To Enlightenment

ISBN-13: 978-0-9940563-5-1

For the ones who are on their last page.

ACKNOWLEDGMENTS

To all of you who I've crossed paths with and to those
who I have yet to, you have my gratitude.

CONTENTS

5 INQUIRY STEPS Q & A

FOREWORD

I must be upfront and confess a long-held deep bias towards any system of spiritual practice that contained a 'method'. No doubt, this was ingrained by my take on, and very long association with, Krishnamurti's teachings, and reinforced by the current small group of so-called radical nondual teachers who stress that there is nothing to do because there is no self who can actually do anything.

However, paradoxically, through the lens of Kyle Hoobin's incisive distillation of the awakening process that he terms 'The Method', I have found that this little book maps very accurately 'my' experiential journey. (And yes, ultimately, there is no journey, there is no self who has taken one… there is no thing. But in the relative, unawake, human experience, there is.)

What's of great value in this book is that it provides a map that closely corresponds to the awakening process. Be it Krishnamurti's story or Byron Katie's story or Joe Blogg's, there are similarities, and 'The Method' reflects this through a methodology of inquiry of five steps. But these are not steps of assumptions or belief-making, but steps that engage the mind to test its assumptions and beliefs, and in the discovery thereof, to die into the unknown.

Kyle Hoobin displays an incredible spiritual maturity in not making any claims for what he offers, but rather invites us to see what's true in our own experience. (He is also extremely pragmatic and asks you not to take on his words if you cannot find their equivalence in your own experience. He is not dogmatic.)

Divided into two sections, one descriptive of the terrain, and the other analytical – the latter through questions and answers that either reflect the workings of the five steps or bring clarity to the mind on particular sticky issues – my sense is that those who are ripe and are exhausted with spiritual seeking and the endless questions of the mind, will find a great resonance with the words herein; and maybe, just maybe, a true catalyst for the final step.

I find that I would have no hesitation is using this book in my academic teaching and research of the transformation model Theory U, which has interesting parallels with 'The Method'. It is concise, and avoids theory for what can actually be discerned in the experiential.

Professor Kriben Pillay
Graduate School of Business and Leadership
University of KwaZulu-Natal, Durban, South Africa
Author of The Poisons—greed, ill will, delusion

INTRODUCTION

I t's been a long journey.

You've searched for a happiness that lasts but continue to come up short. There seems to be a key ingredient that continues to elude you. Why? You're an intelligent, aware human being... right? If there were such a thing as lasting peace and happiness then you should have figured out a way to find them by now.

Perhaps the most bizarre part of it all is that you know in your heart of hearts that there is in fact an end to your search. You can't explain it but you know it. This knowing defies all logic and past experience and yet it can't be shaken. You'd bet your life on it. In fact, you've already placed that bet, haven't you? That's why you're reading this right now.

You're ready to go the distance. You've passed the point of no return and are ready to stake your life.

It's time.

There are five key stages that every seeker of truth and freedom encounters prior to genuine self-realization (enlightenment). These five stages or steps, can vary in duration and intensity depending on who it is that's moving through them. Someone whose suffering is very acute will pass through these stages much more quickly than someone whose suffering is only a mild persistent annoyance. While the duration and intensity of each stage varies from person to person, the stages themselves do not.

The intention behind placing these five stages into book form is to help bring your story and search to a climax more quickly.

By seeing all five stages laid out in front of you, your search will be given more clarity which in turn will solidify your commitment to becoming total in everything you do.

Self-realization without totality after all, is impossible.

You only become total in your search when the medicine of the world can no longer cure you. Only when your situation becomes terminal are you ready to give the truth everything you've got.

The Method is for those whose situation is terminal. It is not a self-help practice. The Method is a guide to help you during the transition from self to no-self... from being asleep to being awake.

The mechanism that keeps you asleep is the delusion of attainment. On a deep fundamental level, you believe that you can acquire an outside source and make it become part of you, make it complete you.

The reason that you can't just read these words and let go of that delusion is that 'you' are also a part of that delusion. The 'you' or 'me' that wants to become free of that delusion is the very thing that's secretly maintaining it. 'Me' is a form of cosmic hypnosis; a cyclical self-sustaining illusion formed from identification with existence. This message comes from beyond that hypnosis but is being delivered and interpreted within that hypnosis.

The value of this message lies in its intention: to render the hypnotized state unfulfilling and thus unnecessary. Only when the hypnotized state becomes unnecessary is it truly ready to end.

If the mechanism of sleep is the delusion of attainment, then why try to help people wake up by using something called 'The Method'? Isn't that a contradiction?

If you are not awake, not enlightened, then it's because you still believe that you can attain awakeness, enlightenment.

OK, I choose to not believe that anymore. Does that mean I'm enlightened now?

You can't just decide to not believe in something, you have to prove that your belief isn't true.

Until you have proven beyond a shadow of a doubt that attainment is an illusion, your 'self' will still feel real and your search will seem justified, necessary, unavoidable.

Taking this into account, it makes no sense to rely on words alone to lead you to truth and freedom.

If proof is what you need, then a process of elimination is what is needed. Yes, this method can only be carried out within the hypnotized state, but once you remove the believability of everything within that state then you're left with no choice but to wake up out of it.

For this reason, enlightenment will not be a result of this method, but a by-product of it.

You exhaust the seeker in you by removing the believability of what is sought. You won't reach for a drug once you know it won't have any effect on you anymore. And even if you do, that tendency won't last very long. So how do you remove the believability of what is sought? By removing the believability of what is seeking.

The usefulness of this method lies in its requirement of single-pointed uncompromising totality through direct self-inquiry.

You can't attain truth, but you can burn through everything that isn't truth.

STEP 1

PROVE WHAT'S REAL

(WITHOUT THINKING)

STEP 1: PROVE WHAT'S REAL
(WITHOUT THINKING)

You think you know. That's the problem. The truth is, you don't know very much... in fact, you only really know one thing.

You don't search, struggle and suffer because of improper knowledge, you search, struggle and suffer *because* of knowledge.

Your suffering continues because you think you have knowledge of something about you and life that's true even though it isn't. So long as you hold your mind's knowledge to be ultimate truth, you will never wake up to reality and you will never be truly free. Your mind IS knowledge. It forms itself from the interpretation and accumulation of life experiences. It's also what you wear as 'me'. The mind is what's trying its best to give you lasting happiness and it's also the very thing that's pushing it away.

What can make it so challenging to live beyond the mind is the original sin you committed when you were very young. What was this original sin? Your judgement of your primary knowledge (what you really are) as not being enough, and therefore, wrong, untrue. If the only thing you actually knew was wrong, then the world of second-hand knowledge became your potential savior; your new best friend.

This is why the first step is to return to your original sight and to your primary knowledge. You can't expect to truly see and truly know for yourself what is ultimately real if you continue to hold your second-hand knowledge as ultimate truth.

Everything you *think* you know is second-hand knowledge. Everything you know without thinking is what you *actually* know.

See for yourself right now. Become quiet for a moment; when your thoughts finally dissolve into silence, notice what knowledge remains when thinking isn't happening. What do you still know with absolute certainty? Eventually, you'll see that awareness of consciousness is the only knowledge that survives this inquiry. This is your primary knowledge.

Navigating the world for practical reasons can require a great deal of second-hand knowledge. To maintain your sense of self and the imagined world that this self inhabits, second-hand knowledge is critical. While you need second-hand knowledge to navigate the world for practical reasons, you don't actually need it to maintain yourself. Maintenance is only needed if something can stop working. Who you really are can't stop working because it doesn't 'work' in the first place... it simply IS.

There's no need to look down upon second-hand knowledge – that sort of thing is helpful if you want to build rockets or pay your bills. There's nothing wrong with second-hand knowledge. Second-hand knowledge has only become an issue because you now use it to tell yourself who you are and how you should be.

Because you have relied for so long on knowledge from outside sources to tell you who you are, it's likely going to take a bit of time getting your bearings straight while you find out what's real.

As mentioned earlier, if your suffering is very acute and conscious, this process will happen very quickly for you. If on the other hand the pain you're experiencing is only just starting to become noticeable, it will be a more gradual process where your inquiry will be at odds with your attachment to your knowledge-derived sense of self.

The mind-made sense of self is obviously an illusion, but why is it so convincing? A more helpful question would be: why are YOU so easily convinced by it? The answer: because you want to be convinced... you need to be convinced. Until you wake up, you won't fully accept the illusory nature of mind because it would force you to accept the unacceptable as being truth: that the only thing you really know is awareness of consciousness (your primary knowledge).

You can only recognize illusion when you stop wanting to be one. Your attachment to second-hand knowledge runs deep. This knowledge is what gives your struggle meaning and justification. After all, you struggle because you know something... something not good.

The first step in becoming free of your struggle is to prove what knowledge is truly yours. You do this by proving what knowledge isn't. By directly scanning the imminent present and ruling out what can't be 100% verified through your direct immediate experience, you return to your original sight and to your primary knowledge - essentially, the knowledge of 'I'.

So let's do a test run and see what knowledge holds up against this scan of the imminent present. Start with some of the obvious assumptions most of us carry:

— *"I have purpose; I have arrived here and this is a momentary stop before I keep moving on"*.

Truth is without purpose because purpose is only possible for that which can become more. Truth cannot become more of itself. Truth never arrives because it can never leave. Past and future have nothing to do with ultimate truth.

— *"I have place; I am an important part of my surroundings and the people's lives I come into contact with".*

Truth has no place because truth is universal and cannot be defined by specific surroundings or by the people in them. Truth cannot be located anywhere specific because truth is everything that exists. You cannot locate everything that exists. Truth is neither important nor unimportant, it simply is.

Then the more subtle object-related assumptions:

— *"I am in a room, I am sitting on a chair, I am reading a book."*

There's no sense in denying that something is happening or that objects exist, just reach out and touch your nose or pick up your cup - case closed. The difference comes in when your label for what's happening and for those objects blinds you from seeing what's really happening and what's really there. Your labels for life are what make up your narration of life. This narration causes you to 'see but not see'. In other words, the story you tell yourself about what you're seeing and experiencing is an act of misdirection.

Then the most subtle of all assumptions:

— *"I am."*

'I' is not an assumption, it's simply, obviously the case. "I am" however is belief-based. The movement from 'I' to "I am" is the transition from truth to story, from wakefulness to sleep. You can prove 'I' but you can't prove "I am". In other words, you can prove that you exist, but you can't prove that you exist as something in particular. This is the key recognition that is needed to guide you through the following 4 steps: If you can't prove that you exist as something in particular then you are not something in particular. Only when the present moment is fully aware of itself is this recognition truly possible.

Obviously, "I am" feels more familiar to you than 'I'. After all, your whole life up to this point has circulated around the assumption of "I am" - of being somebody. The world, the body, the programming you've received from family and friends was (and still is) put in place to reinforce the illusion that you are a separate 'me'. None the less, in spite of how persuasive these factors were, you and you alone were the one that allowed yourself to adopt this illusory identity.

The framework of the mind is its concepts, ideas, judgments, assumptions and opinions. Add all of them up and you have a seemingly concrete reality – a world of information that tells you about the way things are. The Achilles heel of this impenetrable reality of course is the simple fact that you have to be told about it. This world of information does not come from your direct experience (your primary knowledge) which is the present moment. It comes from a remembered past, a conceptualized present and an imagined future. Your direct experience of life has nothing to do with memory, concepts, and imagination though, does it? Direct experience is what you are experiencing without effort, without thinking, without belief.

So what are the implications of sticking with what

you truly know for yourself? How much would change in your life if your life was lived from your direct experience and nothing else? Could you still function in the world? Of course. Your mind is always there when you need it. Want to go to school? There it is. Want to do your taxes? There it is. Want to make a grocery list? There it is. Use it when it's needed... like it was meant for. All we're talking about is not using it when it isn't needed. Want to take a walk? Leave it. Want to look at another human being? Leave it. Want to stop struggling for your survival? Leave it.

Living from your direct experience simply means acknowledging every moment that you're alive by giving your full attention to every moment. Much of your experience of your world and the experience of other people's worlds is one of problems that continuously need fixing because attention is always being given elsewhere. There was nothing wrong with you and the world until your mind came along and decided that things should be better - right now.

Remember: If you face challenges, prove what's real and you will be shown very quickly that challenges can't actually touch your primary knowledge — you will see for yourself that challenges belong only to your secondary knowledge... to your secondary 'self'. Then when you address those challenges you will be coming from a place that knows regardless of the outcome, the peace that you are can never really be touched.

Your primary knowledge is the imminent present. The imminent present is all there really is. In reality, the 'present' doesn't even exist because of that fact. When it comes to ultimate truth, time is a complete lie. 'You' have NEVER been anywhere. You WILL NEVER be anywhere. You ARE nowhere... (now here). These are facts and they will never change. The 'present' changes only in the present, change never happens in a past or a future. 'I' can never be a tense.

So can we describe the experience of this 'I' once all of the knowledge that's been padding it has been stripped away? Not easily. For practical reasons, let's say this: The experience of 'I' is that of an impersonal witness that is aware of the present moment. This witness does not identify with what is contained within the present moment nor does it separate itself from the moment by claiming itself to be a witness. The experience of the witness is not a state of cosmic duality where witness and witnessed coexist, but a realm of being where awareness is brought forth and shines from within everything.

When you first shift from the world of knowledge to the world of the unknown, you will be taking on the role of the witness. Once this shift is almost completed, the role of the witness will be the last thing to go.

Ultimately, truth does not need to witness itself to be itself. Truth is already itself.

STEP 2

WHAT'S REAL COMES FIRST

STEP 2: WHAT'S REAL COMES FIRST

N ow you have a baseline to work with. You know the one thing that cannot be disproven.

While it's one thing to experiment and see for yourself what you actually know, it's a whole other thing to take that understanding and do something with it in your life. You've proven what's real for you — what you actually know for certain ('I'). Now it's time to let that truth sink in and apply it to every moment of your waking life... or rather; to allow the implications of that truth to become evident in every situation you find yourself in. If the only thing you know for sure is that there is an awareness of awareness, then where does that leave the rest of your life? To allow what's real to come first marks a critical turning point in your search for truth and freedom.

To acknowledge truth first in all situations you find yourself in requires utter totality in your commitment to waking up.

But what would that look like exactly? How can you acknowledge truth first when you obviously have a life that needs living, work that needs to be done, people to see and places to go?

Allowing the truth of what you know to come first doesn't interfere with the flow of life and any of its activities. In fact, allowing 'I' to be acknowledged first in all of your activities only amplifies your experience of them. Remember: 'I' itself is already here throughout all activities and experience, so 'you' are not introducing a foreign element into what's happening. What's really happening is that 'you' are being revealed to be what's foreign. 'I' alone is your true nature. The 'you' or 'me' that believes it can put 'I' first is what's actually illusory. None the less, that fact doesn't really change the necessity of bringing the story of 'me' to its climax.

This process of revelation isn't so much an effort on your part as much as it is a willingness to acknowledge the truth that you've already proven to yourself in step 1 *before* you acknowledge any other *supposed* truths about yourself and the world.

Your daily life is now going to become a fully alive science experiment where you acknowledge truth (the one and only truth of 'I') in *every* situation, circumstance and interaction you encounter. Your daily tasks may stay the same, but your experience of them will radically change.

So what does it look like to allow the truth of what you know to come first? Whether you're taking money out at the ATM, making pancakes, having a conversation with someone, driving your car, or watching TV, your passion for truth will acknowledge 'I' first throughout all of these. As a result, all activities will happen within the spaciousness of 'I', as if the 'I' is witnessing everything that's happening.

Any assumptions about anything at all will have to fall under the sword of your verification. Can it be proven right now in this moment? No? Not entirely? Just a little? Then it's not what's actually real.

You are waking up now. You only care about what's actually real.

Here's another example: You get up in the morning. You don't think about the day ahead because you already know what needs to happen. When you pull the covers off, you pull the covers off only. When you put on your slippers, you put on your slippers only. When you brush your teeth, you brush your teeth only. In this way, complete and total focus on *everything* you're doing makes silencing your mind an effortless practice. Through your total focus, your busy dream-generating mind will gradually become unemployed because your attention will no longer be on its content but on the content of what you're experiencing.

Remember: totality is key here. This acknowledgment of truth continuously is an absolute necessity for waking up. Acknowledging truth continuously just means acknowledging what's right in front of you and nothing else. After all, there IS nothing else – right?

Acknowledging that there is nothing else can be made easier by deeply recognizing that it's impossible to leave this moment. It simply can't be done. This moment after all is the only thing that's real. I'll say it again: this moment is the only thing that's real. So if you can't leave this moment, how often do you believe that you can? Recognizing this fact can help silence the mind. After all, what more is there to think about once you acknowledge that past and future are an illusion? There's obviously no need to think about the present, so what need is there to think then? The more this becomes apparent the more you will awaken. Self-realization after all, is the realization of eternity... the truth that exists outside of thought.

The awakened state awaits you in eternity - not in time. Eternity has only one moment - this one.

As you allow this second step to become your natural way of moving through the world, you're going to be confronted with the energetic pull to side with your beliefs. After all, to place what you know first can seem very vulnerable in the beginning because you're placing your trust in something that's essentially a mystery. Place that next to the logic and influence of your beliefs and you will have an unfair match (initially). For this reason, your beliefs about life will likely win over you for the first little while. An example of this might be a bill payment that's due at the end of the month – one in which you currently have no way of being able to pay. Instead of just taking some practical steps to bring in some additional income, you elevate the situation to one of concern because you're assuming the worst will happen; because you're drawing upon your second-hand knowledge. Since this belief is consuming your attention first, what's actually real takes a back seat and you become lost again in the illusory world of a separate 'me' that's struggling to survive.

While the initial pull to side with your beliefs will be strong at first, your earnestness and vigilance in remaining with what's true will gradually shift the gestalt and you will start to feel more at home in not knowing than you will with your second-hand knowledge.

Eventually it will become very apparent that no matter how convincing or real a belief might seem, no belief can survive the reality check that is the present moment fully acknowledged. Your intelligence will eventually conclude that if the present moment is all there is, and no belief can survive in it when it's fully acknowledged, then ALL beliefs must not be ultimately real.

Do you mean that when I leave home in the morning for work, my belief that my home will still be there when I get back is false?

The beliefs that I'm speaking of have nothing to

do with the phenomenal world. The phenomenal world is there whether you believe it is or not. The beliefs I'm speaking of have to do with the illusory world that exists within your mind. Every bit of that world is indeed false. In other words, the thing referred to as a 'house' will likely still be there at the end of your day, but the 'home' that 'you' reside in may not... it all depends upon whether or not mind-identification is still running the show. Who knows, 'you' might leave your home in the morning, a shift in consciousness might take place at lunchtime and pure awareness may return to the house at the end of the day. Anything is possible when truth is given priority.

Allowing what's real to come first means energetically disengaging from not only the story of 'me', but the stories of others as well. You can't acknowledge truth first and energetically support a story at the same time. One has to come second. Those in your life who thrive on your energetic support of their stories may become increasingly agitated by you or even stop speaking with you altogether. Dark doesn't like light. Before you begin to question your sanity and try to reverse direction to try and save a few relationships, just remind yourself that all you're doing is taking your honesty further. You're not judging the relationships in your life, you're simply inviting more authenticity into them. Sometimes that invitation will be welcomed, and sometimes not.

STEP 3

CONFRONT THE DREAM

STEP 3: CONFRONT THE DREAM

Now that you've adjusted to acknowledging 'I' *first* in *every* situation that you find yourself in, the basic framework of the dream that you've created around you will become very apparent.

You see what's been built, so it's time to question its necessity and confront it in yourself if necessary. Let go of believing that what you're getting is not what you're asking for. See what's right in front of you and drop what's serving sleep.

You've established what your primary knowledge is and have made that knowledge your primary concern, now it's time to acknowledge the elephant in the room (i.e., the life you've created for yourself). Acknowledging this will not be difficult to do given that you've already begun to unplug your consciousness from the believability of your life story. When you're allowing what's real to come first, you're allowing yourself to see the mechanics of the dream that you're currently involved in. For example: once you acknowledge that you're sitting in a theatre and not taking part in the movie, the reasons why the characters in the movie are there become rather obvious. You see very clearly that each character serves a very specific purpose that relates directly to the main character. Just as there are no random characters in a movie, there are no random characters in your life. Every person in your life is there to add believability to the story of 'me'. Each person, no matter how small their role may be, is helping to reinforce your illusory self. Does this mean that all relationships are unhelpful? Not at all. So long as you understand that another person's presence in your life tells you absolutely nothing about what you *really* are other than who you've dreamed yourself to be, then there's no problem. How many relationships in your life are there where that understanding is present though? How many of those relationships would last if you were to acknowledge that they are reflecting who you choose to be? For this reason, toxic relationships that are still lingering around tend to not survive this third step. Wolves aren't very enjoyable to be around once you look past the sheep's clothing.

Remember: You've adopted this dream and cultivated the relationships in it for a very good reason - it's given you the sense of who you are... it's made you feel like 'you' exist... even if that existence is a painful one.

The beautiful part about placing what's real first is that you're instantly shown what's healthy and what's not in your life. When you're not perceiving life through a filter of thought, what's right in front of you becomes very apparent. Yes, sometimes it can be unsettling... but so what? You're in this to wake up, not to stay asleep.

By questioning the necessity of what you've dreamed into being, you're going to come up against the core reason for why you adopted this dream in the first place. You can expect this encounter to bring up very deep feelings and emotional wounds along the way.

Is encountering emotional wounds an inevitable part of this process? Yes. Why? Because the truth is, you've dreamed your life into being because of pain - a pain that you've believed must be avoided at all costs. This pain is very old.

When you came into this world you knew nothing. For the first little while this wasn't a problem. You knew that the body responded to your wishes and eventually you didn't mind calling it 'mine'. In spite of this subtle identification that started to develop, life still felt relatively light and care-free. Over time, as your brain and abilities started to develop, an interest in defining who you were began to intensify. After all, you were surrounded by others who appeared to know who they were. They seemed to know what part they were supposed to play. You on the other hand seemed to have a problem; your sense of identity felt incomplete. You seemed to be missing some important piece of information that would explain who you were. You searched for this missing puzzle piece until you found one that seemed to fit just right. Unfortunately, because you were never a puzzle that needed completing, the only way this puzzle piece was able to 'fit' was if it claimed that you were flawed in some fundamental way. And so it went; from that moment on, you knew who you were: a flaw. A flaw that needed fixing. Thus began your search for enlightenment and your departure from innocence.

This search, as you are now discovering, is futile... hence this 5-step method of exhausting the original seeker in you.

By staying with your primary knowledge, you're returning to innocence. You're realizing that there's no way out of your pain so long as you agree that it describes something true about who you really are. You're realizing that only by returning to your innocence can you become innocent... free of being the supposed flaw that you had imagined yourself to be long ago.

Pain dissolves when 'you' dissolve... when you place the truth of what you know first, always. Pain will persist so long as you continue to entertain your secondary knowledge first, as if it were ultimate reality.

Your pain fully dissolves when you fully awaken. To fully awaken, you have to be done with wanting sleep, with wanting to daydream, with wanting to numb yourself, with wanting time. All pain is time-bound. When you no longer derive your sense of self from thinking (time), your SELF is no longer painful.

When you feel that you've fully confronted what it is in you that has wanted to perpetuate the dream of 'me', it's time to allow that dream to end (i.e., yourself).

STEP 4

ALLOW YOURSELF
TO END

STEP 4: ALLOW YOURSELF TO END

By allowing the dream to unravel and by no longer maintaining it, you're allowing yourself to end.

You have recognized the illusions that you've attached yourself to which have kept yourself alive. You've questioned these illusions and confronted them. Now it's time to step off the cliff continuously.

In every moment, life is always asking you if you want to survive or if you're ready to jump. Sometimes the cliff you're being asked to jump off of is small and sometimes it isn't. Perhaps you're stuck in traffic and you're running late for an appointment... the jump is small. Or you've just been told that your father has passed away... the jump is big. In either case, the invitation is the same and so is the destination. So where exactly is this destination? Where you're not; the conscious aware space of pure 'I'. Only in that space can life penetrate your dualistic consciousness and enable itself to dissolve what's masquerading as itself. It's through this penetration that life begins moving 'you' more and more and the personal will starts taking a back seat. This back seat is essentially your will aligning with the will of life (which is whatever happens). As these two apparent wills gradually 'merge' into one, your judgements will lessen and your motives will become transparent.

If you encounter this step too soon it will be because of desire, not exhaustion. You're only ready for this step once you've fully realized that your desires aren't getting you anywhere. You've exhausted any possibility that they will continue to bear fruit. The key indicator of whether or not you've encountered this step through exhaustion or desire is if you're harbouring a pessimistic outlook on life. Pessimism is born of desire – an existential tantrum intended to mask the hope of something better. When your exhaustion is genuine, you'll be neither optimistic nor pessimistic, you'll just know that it makes no sense to want to be something different than what you are.

Given that you've confronted your dream and all of the self-avoidance tactics that have been perpetuating it, your world may start to look like it's falling apart. Relationships may end, jobs may become intolerable, and even your ability to be socially acceptable may disappear. In spite of these seemingly disastrous consequences (resulting from confronting your dream), your yearning for truth will prevail. Your trust in this process of dissolution will be reinforced by your constant returning to what's actually real, to your primary knowledge of 'I' where no suffering is possible. You will know that it's okay for everything to fall apart and for everything to end because you will know that 'I' is the one thing that *can't* end. How could it? You know that 'I' is not manifested and therefore cannot be unmanifested.

Only dreams can begin and end, reality has no beginning and therefore no end.

It's time to accept the reality of the way things are. Through confronting your dream, you've made conscious what was previously ignored. What has been made conscious cannot be made unconscious again. There's no going back now; you either accept that the world you had previously inhabited was for a false self, or you try to maintain that world by ignoring what's been revealed. Keep in mind though that the latter option will only work for a short while. Eventually, even your ability to ignore the light will disintegrate as it becomes far too difficult to blur the line between lie and truth. This slow (often painful) process of letting go can be remedied by not trying to un-see what has been seen when it is seen. Once you recognize illusion, drop it. Don't pretend you didn't notice. The degree of your honesty will determine the degree of pain you will experience. Allow yourself to end over and over again. If a part of you can end, then it wasn't really a part of you anyway.

'You' are the dreamer and you are also the dream. The dreamer and the dream are one and the same. When you allow yourself to end, you are awake within the dream; so what purpose does the dreamer serve anymore? You have seen all of what needs to be seen, what happens next is not your problem anymore.

Now it's time for the last step - to awaken *from* the dream where dreamer and dream are left far behind.

STEP 5

LET GO OF FREEDOM

STEP 5: LET GO OF FREEDOM

Freedom and the lack of freedom is only possible for the dreamer.

The freedom that these steps point to is not a relative freedom, but an absolute truth; a realm of consciousness where mind and its contents are revealed to be an illusion... and thus, duality also.

The freedom that the mind seeks is a relative freedom, which is impossible. The mind wants to be free but only if it can have freedom, not be it. It claims to want oneness but can't accept that oneness means the end of duality... the end of itself. Duality can't become one, it can only give way to non-duality.

The lack of freedom that the mind claims is an assumption that duality is real, was once unified, and can become unified again. Needless to say, the mind's idea of duality and oneness is fundamentally dualistic as a whole. On the level of mind, freedom and the lack of freedom are both illusions. True freedom is the realization that you are not separate from life.

There was never actually a point where you became separate from life – you've only lived a life that has claimed this to be the case. Yes, on the physical level, freedom isn't fully possible while the body is alive. After all, you are the infinite contracted into a finite, seemingly separate thing... a gross misrepresentation of your true nature. None the less, even the apparent dualistic reality of your separate body can be seen through in deep silence. Existence is dualistic, silence is not.

The human bridge to absolute truth is absolute silence. Now you're ready for silence, because...

Now you know what's real.

Now you acknowledge what's real first (the knowledge of 'I') before entertaining any other second-hand knowledge.

Now you've confronted the framework of the dream.

Now you're allowing the dream (yourself) to end continuously.

So now it's time for the core delusion to dissolve. Now it's time to let go of the goal of freedom.

In spite of having implemented the previous four steps wholeheartedly, the truth has remained fundamentally the same (as it always has and always will). What IS fundamentally different now however, is your impulse to seek. It's become severely eroded. The core delusion that time will make things better has all but become extinguished. The previous 4 steps have served their purpose – they've brought you to this place of spiritual exhaustion. You can no longer move forward because you know there's nothing more to see. What started out as a practice: proving what's real, putting what's real first, confronting the dream, and allowing yourself to end has become an automatic process. Those steps are no longer steps for you; they have become the way of sanity.

Freedom can't become the case until you truly stop trying to find it... until the very idea of freedom has been fully recognized *through your own experience* (not through your own ideas) to be an illusion... an impossibility. When this recognition crystallizes, it will consume 'you'... literally. The fire of conscious aware presence is what consumes the mechanism of seeking.

It's through this fire and this fire alone that the very notion of freedom is eventually revealed to be an illusion.

This fifth and final step symbolizes the end of who you think you are. 'You' are essentially the goal of freedom. That's why 'you' end when this goal is finally given up. When you're ripe, you'll stop drawing nourishment from the tree of knowledge that has sustained who you think you are. When that happens, it's only a matter of time before that tree no longer has any ability to hold onto you. You will be let go of. This is why enlightenment is not an attainment. You can't choose to be let go of, you can only stop trying to hold on.

Needless to say, this last step is a non-step. When the time comes for you to be let go of, it will be completely without choice. You will have finally surrendered your will completely to the will of life. The shift in consciousness (enlightenment) that happens after that happens as a by-product of your surrendered will, not as a result of it being implemented. This is why enlightenment happens through grace; a refined space where life is no longer opposing itself, trying to live itself, trying to be itself.

Your last moments as a separate 'me' will be when you stop trying to hold on and life lets go of you. That's when you'll fall. This fall is the mysterious space in which enlightenment happens. An experiential realization of your oneness with all of life flowers here. This shift in knowing who you are is not just an experience, but an irreversible, fundamental transformation of your consciousness.

When the time comes and you find yourself falling,

you won't care to know if or where you'll land anymore. You'll know that freedom is only truly possible when you're falling - not when you're landing.

STEP 1

PROVE WHAT'S REAL
(WITHOUT THINKING)

Q & A

QUESTION:

I observe that my thoughts like to return to certain feelings and patterns with the intention to sustain them. It feels as if this activity of my thoughts is one of the biggest sources of identification because it really feels as if I'm doing it; that part of me is doing this. This part also decides when it's time for a renewal of sadness or anxiety. It feels intelligent, alive and very intimately "me". Is it clear for you? Is it your experience that everything is happening completely without you or a "me"?

ANSWER:

There is no 'me' outside of your thoughts. Thinking feels so intimately 'me' because it can't be otherwise. I talk about the witness a lot... that's a different feeling than the feeling that comes from being in the 'me' state. Resting as the witness is not about witnessing your thoughts (because when you're resting as the witness there are no thoughts) it's about recognizing the space BETWEEN thoughts and rooting yourself there as often as you can. The more you root yourself in that 'gap' the easier it will be to go back there when thinking finishes itself.

The 'journey' to freedom comes into play when you as the 'me' begins to want to remain in that gap more and more often. Obviously a 'me' can't remain in that gap because that gap is only made possible by the absence of 'me'... hence the dilemma of a seeker of truth. You can't witness your thoughts... you can only rest as the witness when thinking isn't happening.

This obviously brings up the topic of free will: Wouldn't you choose to remain as the witness all the time if that's where freedom is? Of course you would. So is it possible to do that all of the time then? No. Why not? Because it's the 'me' (thinking) that wants to remain there all of the time. What you really are is the witness and the witness is ALREADY there all of the time. So freedom gradually draws closer the more you recognize yourself as being the witness rather than the thinker. Again... the witness can't 'choose' itself because it already IS itself.

When the 'me' starts yearning to remain in the

gap between thoughts forever, the pain that the 'me' generates will usually start to become worse. After all, the 'me' wants to become timeless, but 'me' IS time itself. This is why the 'me' in a sense 'dies' eventually because eventually it will realize that it can never become free.

My experience is that experience itself is my experience... it's not 'my' experience anymore though. A realization has happened where what's happening is now seen to be the only thing that's real – as a result, the ownership of what's happening is no longer needed.

Truth is whatever's happening. Illusion is ownership of whatever's happening.

QUESTION:

You say that there is either the witness or there is thoughts. I experience the two to be more fluent, merging somehow. When I realize that I am trapped in thinking, the thoughts don't disappear but the perspective on the thoughts changes. Thoughts may linger a bit and then drop away. After a while new thoughts arise and either float on or pull my identification back into them. The lingering thoughts and reappearance of thoughts feels totally welcome and OK for me, even kind of loving. But this is not possible if there is either a witness or thoughts, exclusively. If that were true, my experience was just a justification for being trapped in a slightly nicer state. Not fighting the appearance of thoughts and hence not trying to be thought-free seems OK to me.

ANSWER:

Throw out everything I say if it doesn't help or if it causes you to question what's working for you. I am your worst enemy if you don't! I would describe the realization that you're trapped in thinking as the moment you recognize that you are the witness. When the witness is recognized amidst the thinking then the return to thinking doesn't have as much of a hold over you anymore, almost like the thoughts aren't as convincing... and if they aren't able to sell you on what they're saying then they will drop away more frequently or 'dissolve' back into the witness. It's like when thinking / thoughts return, the fragrance of the witness is still lingering and too strong to ignore. Definitely not an abrupt thing when thinking switches to witnessing... more like a wave in the water losing its shape and returning to its original expansive state. There were never two distinct / exclusive states. It's all the ocean and the wave is just a temporary appearance of it in a *much* smaller form.

It makes sense that you feel a love arise for the reappearance of thoughts - like feeling love for well-intentioned but misguided children. I made it a point earlier to make a clear distinction between the witness and thinking so that you can more easily recognize the difference between the two - but even thinking is a part of the One, so definitely no need to create a separation where there isn't one. As I mentioned, if my words don't help then treat them as just another bunch of those well-intentioned but misguided children.

QUESTION:

The world is run by egos, they are the problem. They have good intentions but they're really just promising more beliefs – not truth. How can humanity ever wake up when there are so many people who are asleep?

ANSWER:

There are no egos, it's all God. It's all undivided consciousness.

I talk about the false self, some call it the ego, but this 'thing' we're talking about is an illusion that has no reality in and of itself. If you see a human being as an ego, then you are an ego too. When you truly know yourself, yourself is all you see. It's all God pretending not to be God.

QUESTION:

I've been sitting with "Who am I?". It's been driving me a little crazy that I can't wrap my head around what I really am. So it's like I have to sit in this experience and get past the fear of being stuck in a nightmare. It reminds me of trying to bathe a kid who's afraid of the water. You have to soothe them into it. I assume that if I show perseverance and patience, everything will work out in the end.

ANSWER:

You don't need to wrap your head around what you really are — the simple answer (the answer that you've already received) is that you don't know what you are. That is the TRUTH, so don't argue with it. Live by that truth. When you live by that truth, you're forced to acknowledge that you don't know anything else either... you don't know that something is wrong or that something needs to be fixed. You start accepting the suchness of life and start living less from your mind (second-hand knowledge).

This is a great process you're involved in; little processes contained within one overall process. You can liken it to a birthing; complete with contractions and an innate knowing that there IS an end to it... and that the end is worth it.

QUESTION:

A year ago, in a deep depression, I took magic mushrooms and experienced something incredible that changed my life. I have come to think of it as "an awakening", but it was not permanent. What happened was this: the whole world started to collapse and everything disappeared, including space and time, and only I remained. Not "I, this particular body or person" but rather "I, the one who has always been aware, here and now" - it's the unchanging sense of self that has been behind everything all my life. Then it became obvious that I am not separate from the world, and everything in the Universe is literally me. Everyone and everything is just me, and it has always been this way. It was obvious that I am eternal, that I can't die, and that everything is perfect - that this is what the word "God" means. But I also felt that this wasn't the whole story, that this wasn't enlightenment yet.

Lately I've started to wonder about expressions that get thrown around a lot, such as "there is no self", "the I is false", and other things that seem to suggest that even this "I" that remained is false. I wonder if this is in contradiction with what I experienced a year ago, as I would never have said "I don't exist". I would rather have said "Only I exist, and everything else is just me, made of me, experienced as me". Did I misinterpret my realization? Could it be that my ego interfered? Does all sense of self have to go away for enlightenment to be allowed - including the sense of awareness I call "I am" that's behind every experience? Or is the sense of "I am" who I really am, and that isn't going anywhere?

ANSWER:

Drugs can definitely be helpful sometimes (not so much for recreational purposes) to give you a taste of life's deeper reality. The only catch as you mentioned is that it's not permanent. It's becoming aware of something greater at work in life but not being quite ready for it just yet. Enlightenment definitely brings with it those moments, but it's also very ordinary at times. I suppose the difference is that there's no need to take drugs anymore in order for those moments to be brought about.

You raise a really great point: is all of the 'I' false? Of course not. And you know this. As you mentioned, it's more accurate to say that only 'I' exists and everything else is just a part of you. Those who say that all 'I' is false are either trying to say that all identification is illusion OR they are very afraid of the idea of enlightenment and so assume that it's a worse-case scenario where even intelligence doesn't exist.

The true 'I' is VERY subtle though... the full experience of it is only possible in deep silence when there is no longer ownership being claimed over anything. Then the 'I' stands alone... all-one as they say. As soon as the 'I' turns into 'I am' then illusion returns. 'I am' however is simply the human experience - there's nothing wrong with it. There's nothing wrong with illusion. 'I' is the enlightened human experience; when the realization of ultimate truth becomes the go-to place for all 'I am' activities.

You KNOW what you witnessed can be trusted, there's no need to let others' opinions discount that knowingness. Basically, there's no need to complicate something so simple.. something so profound.

Just know that if you yearn to return there then you have to be finished with leaving here.

QUESTION:

I've been hearing over and over through multiple channels that all is consciousness. Science will clearly show that we can never be looking at or experiencing an external object. Any sensory perception is by definition an emergent phenomenon of consciousness. My perception of my body would be as well. Thoughts must also be consciousness. Anything seen/known/ happening must be an emergent phenomenon of consciousness. That's the only way it can be known. Further, any and all things seen/known are "built" of the same substance: consciousness.

Then we get to this idea of awakening and searching/seeking. I cannot stand outside of the consciousness and look in. My writing to you must be part of that dream. My desire to awaken must be part of that dream. My sense of self must be part of that dream. Even my belief that 'I' am in charge and activating all of my life is part of that dream/emergent phenomenon of consciousness.

As I write this I have to realize that any question is just stupid. It's the dream asking the dream how to awaken. That said, I am freaking out a bit because I still feel very much encapsulated in my body/mind. Autonomy feels so real. To switch off the belief that *I* am thinking and move toward seeing that these thoughts, movements, etc are just happening feels almost impossible.

I guess I'm asking if this is true? Is my recognition correct? What does let-go feel like?

ANSWER:

I think I can make this simple; if you have to ask if something is true then ultimately... it isn't.

You have a great mind there, greater than mine I'd say... but all great minds die eventually and so do all great questions / conclusions.

You ask me what let-go feels like... hmm, what would it feel like if you realized that your deepest question could never be answered? ...ever? Who you already are IS the answer but that answer can never be given to the questioner. Answers don't ask questions, they just accept themselves as being enough. Questioners are only satisfied with more questions. Yes, I know in my own experience that consciousness is all there is — when you're ready to accept what you are unconditionally, forever, you will know this too.

QUESTION:

What we really are is awareness. But then there are also appearances; they cannot be separated from awareness, though they do come and go. So what is meant by: "enlightenment is what you really are, and *nothing* else"?

ANSWER:

Appearances come and go, but what is returned to
when they go? Is it a living realization of being aware
nothingness or a sense of self that is being labeled as
awareness? The *nothing else* is the absence of self-
generating labels. In that absence, everything (including
appearances) is seen to be made of awareness (intelligent
nothingness).

QUESTION:

How exactly should one practice something that by itself means no goals and therefore no practice?

ANSWER:

It makes no sense for a seedling to try to be a flower. It makes more sense for a seedling to focus on growth. Yes, the essence of the flower is already contained within the seedling but just because the seedling exists doesn't mean it can just decide to become a flower. Growth is needed first. All growth takes time. Indeed, a flower is no more a manifestation of truth than a seedling is, it's just a full expression of it. So how do you practice when you know that the flower state is one of complete surrender to what is? With the understanding that your practice is to prepare you for total surrender. This preparation is your growth.

The mind itself cannot surrender, it can only develop a practice where it sees more and more of its own limitations. It's that seeing which produces spontaneous surrender more and more. So an effective practice is one in which the mind is shown its own futility - then the mind is forced into silence... but not of its own choosing. Instead of the mind trying to find enlightenment, tell the mind to find itself. Do that over and over again and surrender will gradually arise as a by-product; keyword is by-product. Remember that truth cannot find itself, it can only stop trying to be something other than itself.

QUESTION:

To think that there is nothing one can do to reach enlightenment makes sense to me.

ANSWER:

It's easy for a mind to claim that there's nothing it has to do but not so easy for it to stop claiming.

Enlightenment can only happen when no more claims are being made - even the ones that say there's nothing that has to be done. A constant practice of turning the mind back in on itself and inquiring into its supposed reality removes all claims (eventually). Only then does the debris that covers and conceals enlightenment disappear.

STEP 2

WHAT'S REAL COMES FIRST

Q & A

QUESTION:

You once said that "you ARE let-go." I keep thinking about this and can't quite grasp what you're saying. Can you expand on this more?

ANSWER:

While it's important to play your part by letting go of all resistance, it's also helpful to recognize that what you REALLY are is *already* let go of. In other words, the 'me' isn't really letting go of something and going into something else, the 'me' is an illusion itself and that 'something else' is what's already present. In other words, illusion does the dance of let-go until truth spontaneously appears at the forefront of awareness... but the appearance of truth is not a direct result of the 'me' trying to let-go. A 'me' can't produce truth because truth is what's already the case.

QUESTION:

You've mentioned that the universe exists independently of human awareness. Many experts say that the universe is only possible because of awareness. Or simply, consciousness is all there is. To me this does not say the universe is predicated on a human being present. Only that a universe is made of and by consciousness. Is that your understanding as well?

ANSWER:

Yes, I'd agree that consciousness is all there is and that the universe is not dependant on a human to be present in order for it to exist. That's where the dream analogy (in regards to waking up from 'me') doesn't always match up exactly. Keep in mind (pun intended) that your mind can only view things as separate and so any conclusion you arrive at will be based upon an idea of separation and ultimately unclear and untrue. There is a silent knowing that comes from just resting as the witness, but that knowing only comes through deep silence and as soon as your mind tries to grasp that knowing it becomes muddied. If you are drawing conclusions about the nature of who you are from your mind then your conclusions will always be false. The witness is what you are and it does not need to draw conclusions because it IS the conclusion. Rest as the witness and all that's important as far as revelations go will be revealed to you in good time.

QUESTION:

What about the people in South Sudan who are facing death by starvation or ethnic cleansing? Would you still recommend this practice to parents who are watching their child die of leukemia? Life can be utter misery and pain, no matter what else is happening; such as mass starvation in parts of the world. These are settings of utter hopelessness that we can't possibly understand while sitting behind the glow of our laptops and mobile phones indulging in spiritual ideals.

What fails to bring me peace is the idea that life is supposed to be processed a certain way. I can't truthfully say that "peace" or self-inquiry in ANY context is, necessarily, a more compassionate response than other potential responses.

It feels like a bit of a con job, where if you aren't feeling peaceful, then there is something not right with you.

Mainstream religion tries to justify the suffering in this world as the will of God and that we can't possibly understand the reasoning behind God's will. It all sounds like ignorance of the part that we play in the creation of suffering in this world.

ANSWER:

The events of this world are imperfect and will always be. Life is a constant dance of the negative with the positive. True spiritual awakening is not about eliminating the negative from life, it's about waking up from the illusion that the positive can exist without the negative.

So long as you believe that positive life experiences can exist independently of the negative ones, you will seek to sustain them. You will view the negative as something that shouldn't be happening and will suffer because of it. When you finally realize that the positive can't exist without the negative, you will stop trying to find peace in that polarity.

Needless to say, the key to peace involves transcending your attachment to positive life experiences. This happens when you approach world events with compassion but not preference... when what's real comes first. You know from experience what it's like to believe that life should happen a certain way and so you sympathize with those who still believe that. You know how much suffering that belief can cause. So when you see suffering, you'll help, but not because it's wrong and not because it's right. The more human beings treat suffering in this way the less suffering there will be in the world. After all, the wide-spread suffering of this world continues because most human beings believe that they must fight for what's supposedly right and condemn what's supposedly wrong.

If peace is a goal then it will always fail. Recognizing the peace that arises by allowing what's real to come first is not a con job, it's being awake within the dream of polarities.

QUESTION:

As one drops back into the aware presence and sees the falseness of the story of 'me', a question arises: What about purpose? What about dreaming big, one's intent, pursuing one's joys. Are these all false as well? Or is it that the dissolution of the old personal story removes the resistance toward that which was already inherently wanted?

ANSWER:

The degree to which you are able to drop back into this aware presence is dependent upon how much you believe that your purpose, dreams and joys will bring you fulfillment.

Usually, you only drop back into THIS after you've clearly seen that your pursuits will *always* come up short. You may still be pulled along by your ideas of fulfillment, but if your *priority* becomes recognizing what's real here now then anything else that you believe holds just as much value will become more and more suspect. Why? Because you start to realize that THIS is the only thing that can ever be fulfilling... because it's ALREADY fulfilled. Only fulfillment can be fulfilling. A cup can be filled but it can also be emptied... only an empty cup can never be emptied. Only the recognition of your emptiness can align you with true fulfillment. Only that recognition can dismantle the believability of superficial pursuits.

QUESTION:

Is meditation helpful?

ANSWER:

Meditation can be helpful because it develops your familiarity with that which witnesses life unfolding. The more you witness, the less you are trying to control and the less you try to control the more you are being what you really are. Traditional meditation isn't always the way though. 'Active' meditation, which is just as useful (and in reality, more in alignment with the flow of life), is simply resting as the witness while daily tasks are carried out. When you place what's real first, you are resting as the witness.

QUESTION:

I've experienced that my mind is just a torrent of random thoughts that I have little or no control over. I do have a meditation practice where I stop and try to observe my thoughts during the day but I am still getting caught up in them. I feel stuck.

ANSWER:

Getting caught up in thoughts is only really possible for thoughts. Only thinking can get caught up in thinking. You are pure awareness and that awareness can never get caught up in thinking because thinking can never touch it. So, it's a matter of recognizing the difference between thinking and pure awareness. Directed awareness is not pure because it's confined (has thought boundaries). Pure awareness is that which cannot be directed... it's in a permanent state of witnessing. Your practice has served a great purpose up until now... but now it's time to let it go by going into a deeper recognition of what can't be 'practiced'. In other words, acknowledging the witness as the permanent state and the thoughts as the transient one (not the other way around).

QUESTION:

Wouldn't enlightened Buddhists recommend that you continue a mindfulness practice?

ANSWER:

Practice serves a valuable purpose up to a certain point, but once a person has been doing it long enough there comes a point where it can start to become more of a hindrance than a help. If the intention behind practicing is to eventually become enlightened, then the practice will eventually have to be dropped. Practicing is a subtle form of seeking, and of course, seekers can never find, they can only seek. Practice does help to exhaust the seeker though (which is necessary) so it's helpful in that sense (hence this method). None the less, practice can never bring about awakening directly. If by mindfulness the Buddhists mean recognizing and thus resting as the witness then that's helpful... but if it's about exerting some kind of personal effort to bring about a mindful existence then that's not so helpful.

QUESTION:

I find that I'm intellectually trying to figure out how to wake up. The more I engage my mind in this way, the more I begin feeling the need for a straight jacket. Lately I've been doing my best to stay as 'aware' as possible with 'intent' as opposed to just allowing my thoughts to happen and doing nothing about them. I find that just 'watching' them can get very difficult. My mind is always telling me to do something about these thoughts that I've been experiencing.

ANSWER:

Mind is indeed the ultimate straight jacket; it can only look at things from an actionable point of view. When mind hears the word 'allowing' it can only assume that it's a form of doing... almost like a fail-safe to keep itself in the game. You obviously can't 'do' watching because YOU ARE the watcher (or witness). Mind will always become desperate when you stop feeding it with your attention.

STEP 3

CONFRONT THE DREAM

Q & A

QUESTION:

How did you handle the awakening process while still interacting with your family?

ANSWER:

I never disclosed what was happening to me to my family other than asking for spiritual books for Christmas. There just wasn't a space there where I could share what I was experiencing and have it be received with enough awareness. I knew that they wouldn't really understand what was happening and be able to help me on a deep enough level. Any reassurances I could have received from them wouldn't have touched what was going on inside of me. Ultimately, this was a blessing in disguise; I was forced to see that freedom was never going to come from outside supports.

QUESTION:

Isn't the enlightened experience like the dream model where there's only a single dreamer dreaming? For example, when a character in your dream walks out of the room, you don't assume that they still exist in another location. How is it possible that I am all-inclusive awareness if other experiences exist elsewhere unknown to me?

ANSWER:

There are 2 dreams happening — the microcosmic dream and the macrocosmic dream. There's the little dream of 'me' in which universal consciousness is identified with a human mind, and then there's the greater dream which is existence itself; a product of the macrocosmic aspect of universal consciousness. Regardless of what some 'experts' might think, the universe does exist independently of a human being. A tree makes a sound when it falls in the forest even when you're not around because the tree is just as alive as you are. Everything is consciousness.

When you wake up out of the dream of 'me' you are waking up into the greater dream that is the cosmos. This is why the experience of a dream-state can only truly end when the body dies. Then both dreams are truly left behind.

You are PART of all-inclusive awareness. While this partitioning is ultimately an illusion, it's the human experience and will remain so while the body is alive – even for enlightened ones.

The enlightened experience is that you are not separate from the One (universal consciousness) and that the One is living your life and all other lives as well. It's the experience that everything in existence is made of and by the One.

It's very easy for a spiritual 'me' to get caught up in ideas of 'I AM THAT'. That line of *thinking* requires a subtle identification in order for it to be true. It's safer and healthier to say that you are an inseparable part of the whole rather than saying you are the only creator and all other manifestations in existence are an illusion.

QUESTION:

I have found that some awakened people have a very strong presence. Sometimes when I'm near one it feels like my energy is uplifted and I feel much clearer. It feels like they hold a door open so that I can sense / feel what's on the other side. I've had the same feeling in being with hospice patients; a feeling of being bathed in awareness.

I recently met with a teacher and noticed for about two days after a lessening of my pain and a stronger connection to the witness. Is it helpful when you begin this step of confronting the dream to have direct contact with an awake person?

ANSWER:

An awake person can't cause another person to 'become' awake, but taking the flame of your consciousness and putting it next to one that's burning brightly can sometimes help you to burn brighter as well and work to dissolve things more quickly. Obviously, this can be helpful when you're at the point of confronting the dream since you'll likely be encountering old emotional wounds and repressed feelings.

QUESTION:

At the moment I'm going through a crisis in my relationship. We've been together for many years. The hardest part is that I see myself giving up. I feel like I'm running on empty and nothing makes sense anymore. Is this normal?

ANSWER:

Things only make sense when you think you know who you are. Once you begin confronting your dream, you start pulling the thread on the entire fabric that makes up your knowledge-based life. Everything that you used to find certainty in starts to feel out of alignment; your job, partner, family, friends, society, the world. The reason is simple: your knowledge-based life is a veil intended to blind you from realizing the truth of who and what you are. When you start pulling the thread on that veil, things usually start to become pretty chaotic and disorienting... hence the saying "Better not to start; once you start, better finish." In reality, it's not a choice that initiates this unravelling process – it happens when your seeking has ripened you to the point that you're ready to attract the circumstances that will facilitate total let-go.

Your world may be ending but you know that it's not because you're giving up on it, it's just stopped serving your growth.

QUESTION:

I've been looking for ways to manage the increasing chaos in my life and have found a teacher who comes across as spiritually advanced. Am I silly for being interested in them?

ANSWER:

If you feel that a teacher can be of help to you then by all means try them out. Better to try something out and find out for yourself that it's not a good fit than to rely on someone else's opinion. Having said that, a fairly simple way to gauge whether or not a teacher is genuine is if they help you to realize more of what's already within you as opposed to what's within them. Teachers whose primary interest is themselves usually don't want you to think for yourself.

QUESTION:

I feel so fake most of the time now. I'm going to be meeting up with a group of friends who claim they want truth above all else. I used to look forward to these types of meetings and now it all feels like one big charade. I don't know what else to do so I guess I'll just keep playing my part and saying my lines until I reach the end of my story.

ANSWER:

That's a great barometer for truth... are you being fake or not? 'The end' comes when fake-ness ends. Truth is already here so you can only fake that it isn't. From an enlightened point of view, nobody wants the truth above all else or else they'd have it. Until you're ready for enlightenment your search to become human will continue.

QUESTION:

I'm seeing my projections in just about everyone in the room - and it's so maddening. I went to dinner with a couple of people who tried to talk themselves (and me) into believing that we were already awake just because we intellectually agree with a conceptual understanding of enlightenment and because we all live in the 'now'. I'm suspicious of this conceptual understanding because it still requires me to think about it in order for it to be true... it still needs time for it to be real.

ANSWER:

Your suspicions serve you well. The mind-made 'me' is a time-dependent illusion that keeps itself alive through memory and future projections. It calls 'what is' the 'present moment' because it equally believes that past and future are just as real.

Spiritual people like the conceptual idea of living in the 'present moment' because it offers them some relief from the torment of their false sense of self but also allows them to keep that self alive. When the 'me' is ready to be let go of though, there's no longer any need to 'live in the now' because you realize that there is no 'now'... there's just what is, always.

Eternity (truth) has no 'now' because it has no past and future.

QUESTION:

As I go deeper into step 3, I feel the need to teach others that they should have gratitude for everything and that everything is a gift from the One; that they are a part of God.

ANSWER:

What if there was no one to teach? If you want to wake up, then it helps to question the idea that there are 'others' out there... especially ones who 'know less' than you. It can be a subtle way for the false in you to claim itself as truth.

When you think about 'others', do you know that you're actually thinking about yourself ultimately? Or are you under the spell that says oneness is proprietary?

QUESTION:

My world is collapsing around me. I'm fed up with the thoughts that try to defend or alert 'me'. I feel like I'm always re-living the same pain day by day and that there's nothing I can do to stop it. How can this pain stop? Can it die?

ANSWER:

Yes, the pain can die, but you have to die with it. All that can be left is this moment... are you ready for *only* this moment to exist? The person who is fed up is also a part of the continuous story.

QUESTION:

I used to practice feeling the sensations when an emotional wound was triggered in me, and it was peaceful when I fully allowed them to be there. Now I find that these emotional triggers are happening all of the time regardless of where I am and it's becoming increasingly difficult to feel all of them. My mind keeps reminding me that I am not free because if I were then these triggers wouldn't be there.

ANSWER:

As your willingness to confront this dream intensifies, the painful mechanics that have kept it running will start to surface more and more frequently. The 'me' that keeps being reminded by the mind that it is not free is also mind.

Deep inquiry dissolves the hell. Hell is only for the false. Suffering is only for the false. What you really are is the truth. Inquire into what's real and freedom will be there. True inquiry doesn't require effort, just an openness to recognizing what's actually real here now... forever. It's a passive awareness that aligns spontaneous recognition of no-mind with your heart's desire for freedom.

QUESTION:

You've said that life is never hiding the truth from me; that my external world is a reflection of me. Can you explain what you mean by that? That idea makes me want to scream in frustration... nothing is obvious right now nor is it good. If there's anything that's obvious it's that I'm sick of myself.

ANSWER:

If you say you want to wake up and that you want to be shown what is keeping you asleep then just look at your life. Who do you engage with? Why do you engage with them? Why? Why? Does that engagement foster waking up? Or does it foster keeping you asleep? There is no such thing as being half awake, or half asleep. When it's time to wake up, you stand up straight, look all around you with the eyes of simple seeing and say on the most fundamental level of your being "No more survival."

The self-sickness is important, why else would you want to drop yourself? The self that is sick of the self is all the same self though, it can't drop itself. Only the awakeness that you are can step out of that hell. Sickness persists only for as long you continue to consume something that's contaminated. The only answer now is to rest where you're not. Truth doesn't need to be helped. You are the truth. Be the truth, or be hell.

QUESTION:

Over the past year I've been experiencing strange, often painful physical / emotional effects from this searching. Lots of painful revelations about my 'self' and the beginning of a deep level of understanding (rather than just an intellectual belief) that I'm not what I thought I was. Rather than feelings of love and oneness which I read about, my experiences are closer to horror and terror and (recently) rage.

I can feel everything which I thought I knew about my self being ripped away. The emptiness behind my eyes feels like pure chaos and death. Some nights I lay in bed with waves of what feels like electricity or strong vibrations running thru me, starting at the toe and flowing thru to the top of my head. Some days I find that I'm overcome with horror of what lies just out of my sight. I've also been having moments of complete meltdowns where my whole body is wracked with grief – they usually start with me seeing something that reminds me of my story. I've come to accept many painful revelations about my self but I have the strong sense that there is much more worse things to come. Where's all the peace and light?

I'm convinced the reason that enlightened teachers don't go into detail about what to expect during the awakening process is that their followers would run for the hills if they did and then they'd be out of business.

ANSWER:

I'm sure if someone could ask a caterpillar what it's like after its sealed itself inside of its cocoon it would probably say something like "it fu*king hurts, it's pretty scary at times, my body seems to be changing right in front of my eyes and I have no idea why I put myself inside of here."

Cocoons are not for peace and light.. they're for destruction and rebirth. In reality, you're not moving towards the light, you're tearing away everything that isn't light... and if you try to stop that process once it's begun then fear and terror will have their way with you.

Metaphors like the one above obviously don't give the awakening process any real justice, however, better to use a metaphor to offer some perspective on what's happening then to view the pain you're experiencing as proof that who you think you are is who you really are. After all, one of the biggest traps during the awakening process is to identify with the pain that's being experienced; to turn it into another identity.

Your grief is there to help evaporate what it is in you that's still resisting - there's nothing that quickens the awakening process more than pain that's made conscious. This evaporation is a process of opening your heart to what's happening and what wants to happen, regardless of what it may look like.

Suffering (being asleep) is a closed heart, freedom is an opened one.

QUESTION:

Is there such a thing as a perfectly enlightened relationship? The more that I confront my dream the more that idea is starting to look like a fantasy. All of my relationships seem to be on the rocks.

ANSWER:

There is no perfectly enlightened relationship, there's only allowing love to be as it is. You know your heart, so you know if your heart will stay open or become closed if you let a relationship end or keep it in place.

STEP 4

ALLOW YOURSELF TO END

Q & A

QUESTION:

I can feel the machine, the programming, scrambling to find a foot-hold. I used to keep an inventory of all the great things I had going for me, but lately I find myself coming up with nothing. Now I'm trying to find a spiritual angle on how to handle the despair I feel inside. Now I try to keep an inventory of all of the spiritual advice I received the previous day. My whole coping system seems to be breaking down. The less I feel like I can cope the more I feel like I've been abandoned.

ANSWER:

An inventory... that's a good way of putting it. 'Me' is a continual inventory of the pros and cons of where 'me' is at. No wonder for some business owners, going out of business feels like freedom; no need to maintain an inventory anymore. Letting go of the need to draw from your memory is a powerful thing; after all, what is 'me' without a past? Even though you ultimately don't have control over the comings and goings of your different states of being, you still have a part to play in this great undoing of yourself. In other words, watching your inner world with passivity is important but recognizing the moments when you're being called to "play your part'" is just as important too. You are the state of let-go AND you are also that which is being asked to let go. Life is the puppeteer that moves the strings but the puppet is the one in the unfolding story. 'Surrender' happens by itself but sometimes surrender is an *act* of surrender too.

QUESTION:

Would you define what the tightrope is? I've heard to you talking about that before.

ANSWER:

The tightrope is unique to each person, so I couldn't really tell you what it is for you, only that it's what fuels your motivation to survive. It's the story that you tell yourself about why making the right choice is crucial... or else. To step off that rope means accepting the unacceptable... and only you know what's unacceptable for you. The unacceptable sometimes feels like a dark terrifying void, or something similar; it's the aspect of your consciousness that you've been fighting to avoid your entire life. The tightrope is your method of fighting yourself.

QUESTION:

In most seeker circles I find that people are giving lip service to non-duality, mixing Christian and eastern thought to create a new definition of enlightenment. I see them teaching others that they have a choice as to whether or not they want to be enlightened, as if the personal will holds real power and can produce enlightenment.

ANSWER:

The notion of self falls away in stages, like the notion of choice. For most of the journey the belief in choice can serve a seeker well because it helps prepare the mind for silence (if the choice is to inquire into the nature of mind). Once the understanding of choicelessness and no-mind becomes a deep seated experience then there comes a point when it's time to let the chooser fall away. So to you I will ask... just who do you think 'you' are that you can even make a choice? The chooser is the seed of the seeker. What you really are has no right answers, so making the right choices is an act of futility... it's an avoidance of emptiness; an avoidance of your true nature.

QUESTION:

I've been trying to find where I'm stuck or in denial. There's this track that I've been on where I go around in circles trying implement the 'right' spiritual teaching in order to become free. I was watching a popular non-dual spiritual teacher this morning on my computer; as I was trying to follow what they were saying the thought arose: "maybe if I put all of my faith into this one thing then that's all it will take." I'm so tired of being so gullible. I have the growing sense that this journey has more to do with deepening one's acceptance for the way things already are rather than trying to fix a supposed problem.

ANSWER:

This journey of let-go is much more intimate and drawn out than something that could be easily dropped by just implementing the 'right' non-dual / spiritual teaching.

When my personal story was at its most intense point, I used to sit in the bathtub for an hour or so every day just gently touching my body (in a non-sexual way) making sure that each and every touch was done with great love and respect. Processes and visualizations like that were very helpful in healing the harsh criticisms that had plagued my personality for so long. For a while this helped tremendously and also helped me to become more loving and forgiving of others as well. At the time it seemed like trying to be as loving and compassionate as possible was the whole point of life. After all, how could there be anything else that could trump that? It wasn't until I entered college that even my positive personality traits started to come up short. My biggest problem; the problem of who I believed myself to be (on the most fundamental level) was still there. It was only at this point that I was truly ready to implement a more zen / non-dual approach to things. I realized that no matter how much I could love and forgive myself, my 'self' would still be there and I was becoming more and more tired of having to support it. I realized that finding lasting peace for 'me' would never be truly possible. Only when that became clear was I ready to stop loving myself (by no longer having a 'self' to love). The more I inquired into what was real the less reality 'I' seemed to have and so the less convincing my story became. Eventually, when I was ready to finally, truly, absolutely, unequivocally call off all searches did enlightenment happen.

When I call the 'me' a false self, it's not to disrespect it, it's more to help point out something that's simply not true. 98% of the awakening process is about developing self-love and compassion while the other 2% is about implementing non-dual understandings. Only when your 'self' has learned to be more loving and compassionate towards life is it ready to see that its positive efforts can only take it so far. Only then is the story of 'me' ready to come to an end.

QUESTION:

If a person dies to self and their world is no more, then who is it that is holding the memories, feeling anger, feeling happiness? Who is thinking in the present and relating to others? As I contemplated letting go, I came to a realization that I really truly love myself. I don't really want this me to die. This is the self that greets me every morning and is always there for me no matter what. At the end of every day it is this self that I come home to and makes me feel complete. It's my self that fills my heart with joy and comforts me in sadness. I love myself unconditionally. I have learned to love all of me; the light and the dark. How can I just allow this 'me' to end?

I have been working on dismantling all of my facades and the roles I play to prove my worthiness. I have only recently been able to see the real me and embrace all that I am. The awareness I hear about is an experience of actually being one with all things. I know all is one. I know I am God expressing. My body is matter through which God expresses. Mine has been a work unfolding, sometimes surprising me with the shifts in my expression and perception.

Maybe the problem is that I am looking for a 'knock my sox off' experience where the trees are brighter and the grass gets greener and I am in a blissful void floating around with God.

ANSWER:

It sounds like you've been swept away by a flurry of devotion to THIS and I would not want to, need to, or ever desire to get in the way of that. It's a thing of beauty. I can tell that you now know how to listen to what feels real and THAT is the golden ticket.

You asked if a person 'dies before they die', who is it that has memories and feels feelings? To that I would ask, who is it *right now* that has the memories and feels the feelings? Death is ultimately an illusion, at best it's a word that describes what happens when awareness finally realizes that 'me' is ONLY identification and not a state of ultimate truth. Because to talk of death is to assume that you know what it is, and to assume that you know what it is means that you assume that you know what ultimate truth is. Feelings and emotions are expressions of life but they are not the core of life itself. Positive feelings and emotions are wonderful to experience, but are you at peace when they are not there? Or do you feel the need to have them keep happening? You fear losing touch with positive feelings and emotions when you label them as ultimate truth. Essentially, labeling ultimate truth as something that's impermanent means that fear will be a constant companion. In order to no longer fear losing 'truth', you first have to realize what part of truth can't be lost.

I've realized in my heart of hearts what is ultimately real, but that realization still lives within this form called Kyle who still experiences the spectrum of emotions like anyone else. In regards to 'loving myself'... in reality there is no 'I' AND 'myself'. There is not the

One + Me. True oneness has no companion.

'Me' loving itself can be beautiful, indeed! But realizing that 'me' is not what's ultimately real is even more important because without that realization you will remain at the mercy of life's ups and downs; you'll subtly seek to keep the ups and avoid the downs because there will be no knowledge of something outside of the two.

The truth is in the 'I', it's just not in the 'me'.

QUESTION:

Why would I be given a canvass, if I was never meant to paint... to feel the joy of creating the dark, the light, the colors of all I dreamt could be?

ANSWER:

The deeper human beings are asleep, the darker their paintings. The less asleep they are, the brighter they become. Existence was created more for the painters, not so much for the enlightened. Life after all is a great journey through consciousness; the longer you've been on the journey the more bright and beautiful your painting will be. Eventually though, retirement comes knocking on your door. Your hands become too tired to hold the brush and so all that's left to do is put it down and stand back to marvel at the artwork.

QUESTION:

I'm in the midst of a divorce and the mental/emotional pain I've been feeling has hit a boiling point. It's like I keep getting pushed under the water and then I'm let up every now and then for just a breath or two and then down I go again. NOTHING IS WORKING. Today I felt like I got a taste of something... like defeat only with a sense of peace this time. I've looked at this from a lot of different angles, been involved in self inquiry for years, group self inquiry, friendly confrontation from teachers and fellow seekers. I've tried different ways of asking the same questions because sometimes that seems to help. I have the feeling that the whole surrender thing is useless until it's really time for it to happen.

In the meantime, it feels like there's two levels of pain happening inside of me. One stays with me all of the time; a physical pain in my chest and solar plexus. The other one is deeper and comes and goes; it feels like a pain that has its roots buried in some kind of childhood trauma. I re-read a chapter of one of your books that said when you really face the pain, it dissolves... but that's not been my experience. This feels different, this pain can't dissolve because this pain is myself! It feels like life or death.

ANSWER:

True defeat is a good thing. The fire has been burning in you for some time now and it's starting to run out of things to burn. When the fuel runs out, the fire will extinguish itself. Let the fire burn... it's a fire you can't control anyway. Nothing is working because nothing is supposed to work; dying isn't a movement towards success, it's a movement towards defeat / dissolution. Dying isn't finished until death happens. The pain is not for nothing though... it brings death (birth) closer, faster.

Pain dissolves when you look at it because 'looking at it' is just another way of saying that you're dying into the moment consciously. If you leave the moment (to survive) however, then indeed your pain will be there waiting for you.

Ultimately you are not in control of your freedom but you can exhaust the belief that you are in control.

Surrender is simply the present moment aware of itself and nothing else. In reality, when your awareness aligns with the present moment, there is no 'your awareness' and 'the present moment' anymore... all separation dies. What gives birth to your separation and pain is that you still believe that leaving the moment is possible and that doing so offers you some sort of benefit. Unfortunately, only more pain can teach you how untrue those beliefs really are. How much more pain can you handle? Your pain (all levels of it) is beckoning you to fully die... to not leave the moment anymore.

Your hope may be bringing you up for air

temporarily, but only into a world where you can still be drowned. The moment lived consciously is an aware space where pain isn't; where death isn't, but it's also the space where 'you' aren't either. Ultimately you can't win freedom; it's either freedom or you.

QUESTION:

I once heard you say "You can sense 'your' presence in the eye of the storm because it's the only thing that's still," and "Once that outer storm dies down and also becomes still then your sense of presence suddenly expands to include ALL that is present." It seems like sensing one's presence in the eye of the storm is a nice respite but not really a way to get that outer storm to die down.

ANSWER:

I'll expand on that metaphor a bit more here. There is no way to get the outer storm to die down because the outer storm is fueled by the belief that something needs to die down. YOU are the eye of storm. The eye of the storm can NEVER experience the storm dying down because the eye ('I') is already still. When the eye finally gives up on believing that it's the storm instead of the eye, the eye will only see itself from that moment forward. The storm will then vanish (it won't really die down in that sense). So there's really no way 'to' a state of no-storm, there's only a way 'back' into the eye.

'You' as the storm will never experience peace because the storm is by its very nature a rejection of peace. In reality, the storm that 'you' are has never withheld the truth from the eye, it's only occupied the eye's attention.

You move into freedom by recognizing what has never moved, what can never be moved.

QUESTION:

Did you have a high level of unexplained anxiety before your awakening? Did everything stop working? Did your story take up every waking moment? It's like my ego / mind is in overdrive and I'm pretty helpless to do anything other than watch and feel this terrible mess inside. I don't feel like I can actively participate in any kind of transcendental self-inquiry anymore. I know that I just need to relax into what's breaking apart but as much as I try I just can't seem to get there.

I recall a phrase used by a zen master, he called it "reversing the vector" which is when the tension of the seeking has built to such a high fevered pitch that there's no longer any possibility of being able to turn around or stop what's happening... that surrender will be extracted from you. For some reason 'why' questions have no meaning anymore for me. I'm in a state of high anxiety and discomfort but something is different – like there's a disinterest / dispassionate attitude growing inside of me. Realizing that nothing is going to work anymore has ignited a whole new level of fear.

ANSWER:

Yes, my story took up every waking moment; it was an absolute nightmare. Did I have a high level of anxiety before waking up? Yes, constantly. Was it unexplained? No. I KNEW that I did not want to die. I couldn't accept the possibility that my big problem could go forever unresolved. I did not want to give up which is why the pain continued in spite of how nightmarish it was. I knew deep down that it wasn't just me I'd be giving up on but EVERYTHING. I didn't want my entire universe to disappear into a black hole forever.

Eventually it will just become obvious that your struggle will never yield success and you'll stop avoiding the unavoidable; you'll stop avoiding the void. When you stop avoiding the void, you 'become' the void… the unmanifested eternal aspect of consciousness.

The disinterested / dispassionate attitude is your story losing its momentum as you realize the futility of seeking more and more. This whole new level of fear is normal too; when you've been holding onto the edge of a cliff for a while and then you realize that you're losing your grip the fear will intensify ten-fold. You know that you won't be able to hold on for much longer.

QUESTION:

Last night I experienced an intense state of suffering – almost like a dark, bored, panicked feeling had formed around the edges of my awareness. As this experience started to take me over I felt the urge to DO something. So instead of just staying with that experience consciously, I quickly found something to distract myself. When that kind of experience comes, should I just stay with it and let it overwhelm me?

ANSWER:

It can be easy sometimes to deceive yourself. 'You' ARE your darkness, so when the darkness comes to the surface, the nuts and bolts that make up 'you' are exposed. Whenever they're exposed, the opportunity exists for them to be seen, felt and dissolved. You're right, the feelings can be overwhelming but only for as long as there is resistance to them being there. In reality, only when you can't find an escape route anymore will you allow those feelings to overwhelm you... but it won't be an experience of overwhelm when that time comes, it will be an acceptance of death. If it's not death then it's an unwillingness to die; you've managed to hang on somehow. After all, only a 'somebody' can experience overwhelm.

What you really want to know is if it's safe to go into that overwhelm; if it's safe to allow it to consume you. It's not safe for what's untrue in you... that can't be protected, but that's not worth protecting anyway is it? If you don't go into it, you can't pass through it.

In regards to my own personal story, I don't really remember the pain itself, just that it was bad... very bad. I also remember that the pain persisted only for as long as I felt like my life could still be salvaged... for as long as I felt like the pain could still be 'beat'.

QUESTION:

Law of attraction. Is that pure BS? From what I've gathered after listening to some of your videos it sounds like that's your viewpoint. The way I've interpreted your words is that whatever is going to show up is whatever is going to show up; including one's motivation to say, do, or act in a certain way. If there is a law of attraction (based on how I understand your words), it's basically an understanding that you can accept what is happening now and let go, or resist and suffer.

On the other hand, those who claim there is L of A say that by adjusting your story you adjust your emotional vibration which adjusts what shows up.

How do you see these things?

ANSWER:

Absolutely, whatever is going to show up is what's going to show up. Waking up has nothing to do with making the right choices; it's about waking up out of the hell of choice. It's about consciousness rooting itself in itself while witnessing the mind play it's game of attraction and repulsion... as if that could ever touch the reality of who and what you are.

How can freedom always be present if it can be chosen or unchosen, attracted or unattracted? Freedom is what you really are; you can't choose what you are. If you don't know yourself as freedom then attracting something to yourself becomes not just a play but a necessity... because freedom isn't here... it's over there.

L of A is important for those who want to achieve a certain state of being; waking up is for those who are ready for being itself to be enough. Yes, *sometimes* it can appear that you can adjust your story, adjust your emotional vibration and attract a pleasant experience for yourself, but that's only because your particular story is ready for that type of experience. All choice happens within the story of who you want yourself to be, not outside of it. Choice IS a story.

A helpful inquiry would be to ask: Where does the ability to choose come from? Where does choosing start from? Do you choose to start choosing? Or does choosing just start by itself?

In my own experience choosing starts by itself and then I witness the events that unfold with an aloofness. Sometimes the events that come are challenging and sometimes they're not. Either way the true purpose of each event is to encourage a deeper and deeper let-go into life… to let go of the steering wheel more and more. Those who want to attract don't want to let go of who they believe themselves to be or who they believe they should be.

QUESTION:

Going through this life obediently self-observing in order to hopefully have the liberating moment of enlightenment occur seems like such a waste of time and energy. The only alternative though is to live through a self that is known to be false, smoke, not real. It feels like I'm working on a practice that has no known influence or acknowledged effect on the actual event of enlightenment. In fact, witnessing itself seems to be false now. I can't witness. Witnessing just is. Any attempt to become the witness is itself witnessed. It does NOTHING. It's so frustrating seeing that "I" am useless at creating freedom.

Perhaps this is the end of the road. I cannot come up with anything else to do to wake up.

If I had to guess it would be that either through enough suffering, where the will to carry on becomes unbearable or through sufficient, radical self honesty, acceptance, and scrutiny of mind; ultimate truth will eventually reveal itself. My interpretation is that truth kills the false because the false would never be able to kill itself.

So much angst comes from presuming that I have yet to see the whole truth, because clearly I have not had the awakening that others have described having. I don't know how to stop seeking. I can't stop because I see that I'm not free yet.

Can you offer a description of how you see freedom?

ANSWER:

It's noble of you to search and struggle for this thing called freedom, but it's another thing to be willing to die for it.

The realization of the One is a BY-PRODUCT of freedom, it is NOT the cause of it.

Yes, truth eventually kills the seeker rather than the seeker killing itself... but the seeker could not be killed if it didn't exhaust itself through an arduous search first. Descriptions of freedom do it an injustice but they do help the seeker to exhaust itself... after all, aren't you getting pretty tired by now?

I don't 'see' freedom, I AM freedom... there's a difference. A seeker thinks that if they become free or see freedom 'out there' somewhere that they'll start to feel free inside, but that's a fantasy. That's also why there is so much struggle and suffering for seekers. When the seeker in you finally gives up completely (when the time is right) freedom will realize itself internally first; then (and only then) will that realization become reflected 'out there' in the world. BEING freedom comes first, seeing freedom comes after.

QUESTION:

I can see that consciousness is simply awakeness, awareness, knowingness, a non-thing-presence. Great. Nothing to solve there. Life appears to revolve around this singular point of consciousness.

What I have trouble with is the fact that my rent still has to be paid and it seems like thinking and planning (not being awake) is the only way that's going to happen. So the issue seems to be that, yes, you can recognize what wakefulness is but so what? It seems a bit naive to think that once enlightenment happens that everything is going to be hunky dory and that the universe will just pay your rent for you.

If I give total attention to the moment continuously, forever; will life provide for and take care of this body / form? How is anything going to get done? I feel like I need proof in order to be able to trust. I think my guard is up all of the time because I think that life couldn't care less if this body / form lives or dies.

ANSWER:

How is anything going to get done? Well, how is anything getting done already? If the false self is false, it means that it's never truly gotten anything 'done'. It means that what's happening is always a product of truth... even if truth is wearing the mask of the false while it's happening. So it's not about figuring out how to get things done while trying to rest as the truth, it's about deeply recognizing how things are *already* getting done. You don't bring awareness into the present, awareness IS the present. 'You' are not brought into the present, you ARE the present. When awareness becomes aware of itself, 'you' are absent. Awakeness becomes the case. Awakeness is what witnesses the unfolding of any doing that's happening... it also 'becomes' the doing at the same time. There's no separation between witness and doer. The moment that life recognizes itself unfolding, it's awake.

Life always wants to support itself... but if life (you) believes that it's separate from itself then its support will not be recognized when it's given and may even be labeled as a threat.

Realizing / recognizing the wakefulness that you are and giving your attention to THIS is what enables life to start supporting itself again because it's gotten out of its own way. When the knot (not) that is 'me' becomes untied through continuous recognition of wakefulness, life's natural supporting functions flow freely without restriction.

Yes, rent gets paid by thinking and planning but that's not an issue if awakeness has realized that it's not a thinker or planner. When awakeness realizes that it's not a process of thinking, it can pick up the time-bound tools of thinking and planning with playfulness... not serious life or death determination. When life is truly awake to itself, it knows that thinking is not really what takes care of itself. The hand doesn't need to think before it can feed the mouth.

Q & A

QUESTION:

You speak of deep silence as being ultimate truth; is this something that you abide as or does it come and go? Based on my personal inquiry I would assume that deep silence cannot be 'done', rather your essential nature becomes recognized AS deep silence? If deep silence comes and goes that would mean that at certain times self is the assemblage point and other times silence is the assemblage point. Is this your experience?

ANSWER:

There's the silence you realize as being the background of all experience (your true nature) and then there's the silencing of the mind (which can fluctuate / come and go). To wake up is to realize yourself as that background. Mind will still fluctuate, but when you truly know yourself as not mind then you will also know that those fluctuations can't really touch what you really are. What you really are never comes and goes. It's the difference between watching a show on the TV and believing that you're in the show. Mind is TV, truth is what's watching.

QUESTION:

I'm tired of trying to figure all of this out.

ANSWER:

There comes a point when the mind can no longer answer its own questions. At some point, simple pure awareness has to take over and be given priority over the mind's need for answers.

QUESTION:

There seems to be an in-between state where I'm just okay; kind of neutral. It's this place that's peaked my interest; what causes me to go from extreme pain to neutrality and back again? Does some thought process stroke my sense of self into feeling better? It feels like this is what we do all our lives; constantly doing maintenance work to make our 'selves' feel better. I feel like I'm being torn apart inside but the fear that says my whole life is going to fall apart is being seen through more now. Parts of my life have already fallen apart and it's still been okay for the most part. I still feel like I'm in over my head though and to make matters worse I've been getting 'talks' from my family members who are recommending that I get some 'help'.

It feels like my ego is out of control, scared and backed against a wall. How can an imaginary fantasy cause so much anguish?

ANSWER:

Either we work to make and maintain a self or we don't... deceptively simple.

Any idea of arriving anywhere into any kind of future state is an illusion. Enlightenment is an amazing and profound transformation of consciousness, but it's a realization of what's already here.

You're stuck with where you are forever... but is where you ARE able to actually experience suffering? Isn't it when you claim ownership over where you are that suffering arises? As long as you still think that you can 'own' where you are, suffering will keep paying you a visit. The world (including your mind) can only see you and know you as a time-bound being with a past and a future who's in the midst of struggling or succeeding at something. The world can NEVER know or understand what you really are because you can't be located anywhere or identified by any means. How can you pinpoint aware emptiness? Death is not an event that you can own, it's a willingness to let go of ownership for good. Notice that you don't need to own the present moment... it won't go anywhere if you stop owning it. What you REALLY are can't go anywhere or be touched by any struggle... or be 'owned'.

'Me' is an illusion. Unidentified consciousness (pure awareness) is what's real, so consciousness trying to get rid of the 'me' is an attempt to get rid of something that doesn't exist. It can't be done. Obviously, this 'me' seems very real and the suffering experienced as a result of this apparent 'me' makes it seem as though there really is something that needs to be gotten rid of. None the less, 'me' is a conditioned illusion; a contraction of awareness. This means that there's nothing to grab onto that can be thrown away. The only thing that dissolves illusion is continual recognition of truth; of the moment; of the space where 'me' doesn't exist.

Q & A

QUESTION:

I'm stuck. I don't know what to do to end all of the pain and I don't think I should do anything because doing something will only get me further away from my goal. I don't think I should even have a goal! You know what I mean?

ANSWER:

Truth is always stuck, it can never go anywhere. You however are not stuck, you still think you can go somewhere, attain something. That's perfectly normal and that's why the pain is still with you. Pain can only survive for as long as it has room to move around in. There's no room for pain in truth because truth can't move an inch so it can't make room for anything else. Pain needs your past and your future. Truth has no past and future. Truth is timeless, pain is time-bound.

STEP 5

LET GO OF FREEDOM

Q & A

QUESTION:

Can you give me an idea of what the run up to your awakening was like? Was there a buildup of painful emotional waves before it happened? If so, how long between waves? Any nausea? How did you feel a few seconds before your awakening? How did you feel a few seconds after?

In one of your books you say that you were picking up a bucket or something and then something released inside of you; how did you perceive your environment before and after that happened? You said that everything appeared sacred, what does that truly mean? Sacred to me is graveyards, temples, churches, religious paraphernalia, angels, chanting and the like. How can a bucket appear sacred?

ANSWER:

I started my search for freedom when the pain inside of me started to intensify (around the end of elementary school and beginning of high school). In a way, my 'spiritual' search started by looking into new-age things and discovering the practice of self-inquiry. This practice of self-inquiry helped sensitize my 'being' to the lightness of the present moment. It can be likened to dipping your toe into a warm bath and then gradually sensitizing the rest of your body to the temperature of the water.

By the time I reached 20, my story of suffering had reached a boiling point and my 'beingness' had sensitized itself enough to the present moment that I was ready to 'merge' with it. The event with the bucket was the climax of my story. Yes, I experienced waves of emotional anguish leading up to my awakening. The frequency of those waves intensified as I moved through high school to the point that there was very little space between them anymore. Sometimes these waves brought on physical sickness as well.

How did I feel a few seconds before the awakening? Exhausted.. totally utterly exhausted. It became crystal clear that the end had come. I didn't know what that meant at the time, just that I didn't have it in me to seek out a solution anymore. How did I feel seconds after? Perplexed, in awe, at peace. How did I perceive the environment before and after? Before, 'Me' was still there and so 'me' was where the focus was, not on the environment. The environment was already labeled and 'known' so I never really saw it. After, 'me' was not the focus anymore and so existence was all that was left... labels fell away. IT awoke to itself and could finally see itself... hence I say that everything suddenly appeared sacred; IT realized that everything was IT, everything was intelligent, everything was full of this intelligent presence... even a bucket. Sacredness is not in the things or ideas that we assign specialness to (like temples, churches, religious paraphernalia, angels, chanting), it's in recognizing the God-presence in everything that exists... EVERYTHING. Recognizing that presence in everything is only truly possible in deep silence, which is why 'me' blinds most people from seeing it. 'Me' is ignorance of silence. Everything that exists is sacred because it's all made from One universal, eternal, intelligent awareness.

QUESTION:

I've heard one teacher say that when they woke up they realized that they were what was behind everyone's eyes; that they were literally, actually behind everyone's eyes. Is this what you mean when you talk about the realization of oneness?

ANSWER:

I can't see behind other people's eyes. If what this teacher was trying to convey is that the source of every human being is pure undivided intelligent awareness and that that undivided awareness is what's behind all eyes then that makes sense to me. I can't feel another person's feelings directly but I can deeply sense / sympathize / empathize with another persons feelings. It's very misleading, unhelpful and untrue to say that you can own another person's experience. The truth is that you are a PART of ALL that exists. The enlightened human experience is not that you can suddenly experience what every other human being is experiencing, it's that you recognize that all experiences and manifestations in existence originate from One consciousness. There's a great saying…. "A buddha gets hungry in his belly, not in yours."

QUESTION:

I started my awakening a few years ago when I realized that I wasn't just a human being anymore, but instead One consciousness behind everything.

There's one nagging thought that's been eating away at me though. How can I know if my awakening isn't just another trick of my brain? After all, the brain works by creating a holographic projection of the world based on the flow of electrons coming from the sensory organs of the body. So what if 'awakening' is just the brain breaking down one's sense of self to the point of seeing the hologram as 'one' hologram. Maybe I don't really see all of reality as One but instead see all of my own hologram as One.

How can I know that I'm not just delusional?

Maybe I'm just the first 'awakened' person who has ever considered this?

Right now, the only way I've been able to make peace with this is to find a flaw in my thoughts or to accept that I will never know the answer.

ANSWER:

Your awakening has not penetrated deeply enough yet. You still believe that awareness is the same as intellectual intelligence. Enlightened awareness is not the same thing as a thought process. Enlightened awareness is a singular knowing, not a dualistic one. All thoughts are dualistic. True enlightenment reveals that undivided awareness is the ground of all phenomenon; it's the unmanifested reality from which all dualistic experiences arise. In other words, if it's authentic, enlightened awareness is not something that can be subjected to debate by a thinking mind.

As you said, thought is a clever trap of the ego... thought IS ego. There's definitely a common tendency in many who awaken to identify with awakening itself and then label their experience as something that can be identified with. It's certainly delusional, albeit a more refined and less suffering-based form of delusion.

Seeing oneness is not delusional though, telling your 'self' that you're seeing oneness is. I talk about seeing oneness a lot but that's only because I have no other way of pointing to something that can't be pointed to. Talking about oneness is the same as pointing to the moon's light to tell you about the existence of the sun.

Going into thoughts about holograms and brain function is definitely the false self (which is any self) trying to conceptualize awakening. It may seem like honest scientific inquiry, but so does seeking for anyone else who has not woken up. The moment of awakening is a moment of complete and utter let-go; a total willingness to let go of all knowledge. You realize that you are the source of knowledge and that knowledge itself comes after you. If you'd like to lay your question to rest and be at peace, then you have to step back into THIS space of not-knowing, not-identifying, not-being. In that space of not-knowing a deeper knowing will gradually become evident, only it will be a knowing that is only known unto itself.

QUESTION:

I've always been fascinated by death. Before I encountered people who were 'into' enlightenment teachings I found my community with the dying. I've worked with the elderly for a number of years and have had the same energetic experience around certain awake teachers as I've had around the dying.

I've never really been concerned with where I go after death, my real fascination is: where does all of this go when I die (my home, children, the world)?

ANSWER:

Leave physical death to the physical. As far as false-self death goes, your home, children and the world remain; the main difference is that your relationship to them changes... or rather, it ceases. Not that you stop relating to others and your environment, but that the illusion of believing you are a separate 'somebody' relating with other separate 'somebodies' ceases. You realize on a deep level that there are no relationships in the traditional sense when it's only ever the Self interacting with itself. All relationships become sacred.

When the false self dies, everything remains but it's the remains of one, not two. There's no longer 'my' home, 'my' children or 'my' world... there's home, children, world and IT recognizing that IT is all of those things. The beauty and intimacy of life remains, always.

QUESTION:

You and I very briefly touched this subject a while back but you chose to not answer my question. Your reason was that no answer would be satisfactory. I'd like to ask you again as it's a sticking point for me. You've spoken of fundamental silence before and that you see God everywhere. Can't this silence and 'God vision' just be a basic running program of the brain or something similar? After all, neurological studies can literally turn off speech, movement, time perception, memory etc.. The enlightened argument is that these alterations still have to be observed by something. Obviously this would mean that awareness is still present; that awareness can't be turned off. The test for that of course is death. But how can anyone verify the result of that?

ANSWER:

I once told you that I see God everywhere. That statement is true but it's also misleading in a way. I don't 'see' God in the traditional way you would think of seeing something. When I initially turn my attention to a particular object and look at it, I'm using my brain to do that. Once my attention is on that particular object however, I can stop looking at it even though my eyes are still directed towards it. This 'stopping' of looking at something is the same moment that God reveals itself in the object I was previously looking at. This 'stopping' is what I can't put into words for you... but essentially it's the same as a kind of death; the function of seeing stops and in that stopping perceiver and perceived fall away and what is revealed is an inherent intelligent presence.

The brain needs time to function - it only works by connecting point A to B to C etc. which is how vision works (light is transmitted to the eyes which send that information to the brain. The time it takes for that to happen is what creates the illusion of perceiver and perceived. It takes time for human vision to happen.

Enlightenment is seeing reality outside of time. When that happens reality sees itself. No light is being transmitted to the brain (because time has completely stopped). The light that was previously being transmitted now has nowhere to go; it can't travel anymore and because of that all 'objects' shine unto themselves. The enlightened eyeball analogy is helpful here: the eyeball realizes that the only way to know itself is to stop trying to look at itself and just start being itself. It's in that 'beingness' that a different kind of seeing takes place, one that doesn't need light transmitted in order for understanding happen.

As you said, death is the only thing that can verify what I'm saying. Death can indeed happen while the body is still alive by aligning your consciousness with the timeless... this eternal instant.

Before enlightenment, when you look to the present moment, you can sense 'your' presence but you don't necessarily sense that presence anywhere else because you're just resting in the eye of the storm for a moment. The storm is your busy, fear-motivated mind; it blinds your presence in all 'other' things from you; it keeps you in time. Enlightenment finally happens when light stops travelling and starts being... everywhere. When that happens, the functions of the body become something that you can smile at but not put much stock into (as far as telling you what's ultimately real).

QUESTION:

The idea of enlightenment confuses me. Obviously
there's something profound that shifts in a human being
when it happens and yet so many teachers say that the
true Self (the divine Self) does not become enlightened
because it's already one's true unborn nature. It sounds
like enlightenment is only a dramatic change for the
human mind / being, but not for consciousness itself.
Is this right?

ANSWER:

I understand that the idea of enlightenment makes no sense when trying to understand things from a non-dual perspective. After all, if all is one, then who becomes enlightened? On the deepest level, undivided consciousness is all there is. This is the untouchable reality of eternity. On the human level, human awareness is evolving in consciousness, gradually transcending mind, gradually returning to its original resting ground of pure unidentified awareness.

Another way to look at it is like a seed; a seed and the flower it becomes are made of the same stuff, their essence is one but the state of a seed and the state of a flower is obviously very different. Ultimately, a seed that grows into a flower doesn't add anything more to truth, it just becomes a fully manifested expression of truth. Enlightenment is a flowering after a long period of growth in consciousness. When an enlightened person leaves this earth, the great dance of growth comes to an end and the consciousness that flowered is ready to return to itself as the everything.

QUESTION:

What is Nirvana? Is it a place? Does bliss come into it? And if so, is it constant?

Would it be right to say that awakening is a kind of 'blending' with the infinite? When one wakes up, what is important to them?

ANSWER:

Nirvana is when you no longer leave this moment. In reality, it's the only place there is. Yes, bliss comes into it sometimes but it's not always constant. What makes Nirvana Nirvana is that you realize WHO YOU ARE is a peace that can never really go anywhere; that it has never really left you; that it could never really leave you. You could never leave you. Sometimes this peace encounters joy, bliss, agitation etc., but what's most important is the peace that can't be touched; the peace that can NEVER leave.

You could say that there is a 'blending' or 'merging' with the infinite, but the truth is that there is nothing that can merge because there's 'not two'. That's why enlightenment is dying the deathless death; it's the dissolution of the great cosmic hypnosis called duality.

When one wakes up, nothing AND everything is important. You understand that ultimately real reality can never be destroyed and yet you have great compassion and appreciation for this great play even though it's only temporary. So what's 'important' is whatever you assign importance to. The appreciation for all of THIS also has a kind of importance to it, though it's not serious.

QUESTION:

People with egos who are not prepared to understand truth have great difficulty with the concept of living in the moment. How do you help them?

ANSWER:

Don't even go there anymore. Talking of egos gives reality to egos, it reinforces the illusion that you are separate from life and that life is separate from you. It makes it seem as though an 'ego' is separate from you.

I could choose to see Bob as "Bob, the guy with an ego" but doing so means that I'd separate myself from him and so I'd end up with just as much of an ego. Being awake means only seeing what's awake. Yes, other humans are playing the sleeping game but recognizing their awakeness is what's most important; otherwise you put yourself to sleep by believing that sleep is reality; that separation is reality.

QUESTION:

I don't understand how it's possible to surrender and at the same time practice and have a goal. Isn't it true that the more I practice and cling to this goal of enlightenment the further away from enlightenment I get?

ANSWER:

Nothing can push you away from enlightenment because enlightenment is not an attainment, it's a dissolution. The more you practice, the more you exhaust the seeker in you. When you are fully exhausted, you dissolve into enlightenment. You don't become enlightenment, enlightenment finally stops being something other than itself.

QUESTION:

Isn't enlightenment a state of no desire?

ANSWER:

Yes and no. Yes in that you realize that your true nature is what is most fulfilling and that nothing could ever compare. No in that doughnuts are still delicious and spaghetti is a wonderful way of filling a hungry belly.

QUESTION:

Isn't enlightenment a state of complete surrender to what is?

ANSWER:

Yes and no. Yes in that enlightenment is a realization of what you really are, and that what you really are can only be seen through deep surrender to what is. No in that emotions can still arise and cause resistance to what is sometimes. The main difference is that you no longer mistake ultimate reality to be a state of emotion anymore. You've realized that emotion isn't the ocean, just waves on the surface. Enlightenment helps you to reside as the ocean more which means that the waves become less frequent, less turbulent.

QUESTION:

Isn't enlightenment not wanting things to be different from what they are?

ANSWER:

Yes but so what? A seedling still has growth (preparation through exhaustion) to do before it's ready to flower (totally surrender).

QUESTION:

Isn't enlightenment a state in which one accepts pain and suffering?

ANSWER:

There can still be pain after enlightenment but suffering is only possible through identification with pain (building a personal story around it). Enlightenment is the end of stories.

QUESTION:

I find that I'm always getting stuck on trying to figure out the origin and nature of mind.

ANSWER:

Inquiring into the nature of mind is helpful but the origin not so much. Finding out its supposed identity here now wakes you up, finding out what created it doesn't.

Understanding the origin of mind comes in time. Suffice it to say that when consciousness emerges through a human form, the climate for identification is perfect; consciousness is given interests through feelings and a body that responds immediately to the wishes of those interests. Everything that's given (the body, interests, feelings) serves to create the hypnosis that is 'me'. Just as a country is an illusion and nothing more than the conceptual sum of its parts, so too is the mind an illusion and nothing more than the conceptual sum of what is given from the time of birth.

That which gives these parts is the truth, the creator, source, the void. This giver remains a mystery until these parts are fully removed (physical death). This is the case even for enlightened ones.

Mind creates nothing because mind is an illusion, a hypnosis.

'You' are a manifestation of the creator AND because of that, you are the creator manifested. Your will exists not because 'you' choose for it to, but because it's always being given to you. There is only One will, not two.

QUESTION:

Is enlightenment the same as death? Does it happen when there's a death of identification with 'me'?

ANSWER:

Identification can't die because identification is not a 'thing'. Only things can die. Enlightenment is when identification dissolves; it's a deathless death... the death of a contracted sense of self called 'me'.

When a hypnotized person comes out of hypnosis, did their hypnotized self die or did the illusion of that self simply disappear?

QUESTION:

I've had the shift in consciousness that's referred to as enlightenment. One afternoon, several years ago, while feeling psychologically sick, I had a transformative experience where something deep inside of me gave up. Shortly after I noticed that everything was alive with presence; with 'my' presence.

The intensity of that initial experience has since subsided, but it was, and still is, seen that everything is awareness. I still feel like there is a sense of self present though, almost like a thinker that should not be present. While intuitively I know that this feeling arises from a fear-based thought and so is ultimately untrue, the feeling is none the less a persistent one. Is it possible that I'm still not completely done?

ANSWER:

I've mentioned the fan-blade analogy before. What I've come to observe and experience is that after someone wakes up there are still echoes of the old self that take time (often years) to slow down and fade away. The fan has been unplugged but it's blades have some momentum left in them. For some, this slowing down process can happen rather quickly and for others not so much.

From what you've described, it sounds like you have woken up, so you now KNOW experientially that death is an illusion and that fear has no ground to stand upon anymore. This means that any echoes / thoughts of a 'self' that are still present are going to dissolve in due time as you continue moving through various life experiences. The good news is that because you now know that death is an illusion (and have the 'vision' to accompany that knowing), it's far less difficult now to be willing to die over and over again whenever life asks you to.

It's been well over a decade now since I woke up and in that time I've encountered many challenging / difficult life situations. All of these challenges have worked to chip away at any attachment to 'self' that remains. In other words, my fan blades have slowed down considerably since I first woke up but I can still feel some movement there from time to time.

You know that ultimate reality is already 'done', it's the gradual fading away of the deeply programmed belief that you can 'be done' that takes time.

You are home now. Life will still have its ups and downs, but you are home now.

IN CLOSING

If there's anything worth taking away from this book it would be a validation that ultimate truth exists.

If that suspicion has been validated (even just a little), it means that your life is forever changed. There's no going back now. Now you know that life is not just made up of a series of relative truths that can change from person to person, moment to moment. Now you know that accessing this absolute truth is possible for anyone who's willing to become total in their search for it.

The game is weighted in your favor now... what happens next?

Kyle

ABOUT THE AUTHOR

KYLE HOOBIN is an author, photographer, graphic designer and self-inquiry teacher.

In April of 2002 Kyle experienced a profound shift in consciousness following a long battle with depression. He now offers support for those seeking authentic freedom in their lives.

Kyle's teachings focus on practical and accessible methods of self-inquiry with a focus on finding freedom through direct personal experience. He has distanced himself from conventional lineage based teachings in an effort to establish a more authentic spiritual standard for spiritual seekers.

To learn more, visit kylehoobin.com and take part in Kyle's monthly live streams and self-inquiry videos.

VISIT:

WWW.SIMHASATPUBLISHING.COM

FOR MORE GREAT TITLES!